WITHDRAWN

A KID'S GUIDE TO THE
X Games™

IN-LINE SKATING

in the
X Games

CHRISTOPHER BLOMQUIST

The Rosen Publishing Group's
PowerKids Press™
New York

For two Xtremely wonderful nephews, Timothy and James

Safety gear, including helmets, wrist guards, kneepads, and elbow pads, should be worn while in-line skating.
Do not attempt tricks without proper gear, instruction, and supervision.

Published in 2003 by The Rosen Publishing Group, Inc.
29 East 21st Street, New York, NY 10010

First Edition.

J 796.21
B

Editor: Nancy MacDonell Smith
Book Design: Michael de Guzman and Mike Donnellan
Layout: Nick Sciacca

Photo Credits: Cover © Icon Sports Media; p. 4 (top) © Getty Images; p. 4 (bottom) © CORBIS; pp. 7, 8, 11, 15 © Tony Donaldson/Icon SMI; pp. 12, 19 © Zach Podell/Icon SMI; p. 16 © Ezra Shaw/Allsport; p. 21 © Photo by David Bartolomi.

Blomquist, Christopher.
In-line skating in the X Games / Christopher Blomquist.— 1st ed.
    p. cm. — (A kid's guide to the X Games)
Includes bibliographical references and index.
Summary: Introduces the people and events connected with the aggressive in-line skating competition that has taken place twice a year since 1995 at what is the Olympics of extreme sports, the X-Games.
  ISBN 0-8239-6302-0 (lib. bdg.)
1. In-line skating—Juvenile literature. 2. ESPN X-Games—Juvenile literature. [1. In-line skating. 2. ESPN X-Games.] I. Title.
  GV859.73 .B64 2003
  796.21—dc21

10/03
American Kids
19.33

                                                                                2001007977

Manufactured in the United States of America

Contents

1   What Is In-Line Skating?   5

2   In-Line Skating at the X Games   6

3   Picking Skaters for the X Games   9

4   The 1ˢᵗ X-Games In-Line Competition   10

5   Great Moments at the X Games   13

6   A Star In-Line Skater at the X Games   14

7   The Park Event   17

8   The Vert Event   18

9   A Talk with Matt Lindenmuth   20

10   What's Ahead for In-Line Skating   22

      Glossary   23

      Index   24

      Web Sites   24

4 *An old-fashioned roller skate is like a car. It has a pair of wheels on both of its sides. The wheels on an in-line skate are in a straight line, like the blade on an ice skate.*

What Is In-Line Skating?

In-line skating is a form of roller-skating. In one type of in-line skating, the skaters do bold tricks. These tricks might be jumping off ramps at high speeds and doing **midair** spins and flips, or skating down a set of stairs. This kind of skating is called **aggressive** in-line skating. Aggressive in-line skating is the only type of in-line skating that is done at the X Games. The sport got its name because to be aggressive is to be bold. Even the boldest skaters know to wear a helmet, knee pads, elbow pads, and wrist guards while skating. This gear protects them from getting hurt if they fall.

Aggressive in-line skating is an **extreme sport**. Extreme sports feature a lot of risky moves and are newer than sports such as baseball or basketball. Extreme sports are also called action sports.

5

In-Line Skating at the X Games

The first Extreme Games was held in 1995, in Rhode Island. The next year, in 1996, the **competition**'s name was shortened to the X Games. Today the X Games are held twice each year, once in the winter and once in the summer. Extreme **athletes** try to win **medals** and prize money at the games. At the 2001 summer X Games, a total of $1 million was awarded.

Aggressive in-line skating is a summer X-Games sport. The sport has been an X-Games men's and women's sport since the first games, in 1995.

History shows that in-line skating is definitely the most **international** sport at the X Games. Over the years, most of the X Games's in-line champions have not been North Americans. For example, star in-line skater Fabiola da Silva is from Brazil.

6

Chris Edwards is an X-Games medalist. Edwards is from Minnesota, but most winning in-line skaters at the X Games come from South America, Europe, Australia, and Japan.

Iain Smith does a flip for the judges at an ASA Pro Tour event in Philadelphia, Pennsylvania, in 1997.

Picking Skaters for the X Games

The **Aggressive Skaters Association** (ASA) oversees aggressive in-line skating at the X Games. This group decides which skaters to invite to the X Games each year.

For the men's events, the top four finishers from each in-line event held at the most recent X Games are asked back. Others **qualify** by placing first in six ASA Pro Tour events held in the United States and Europe. The winner of the Asian X Games Qualifier, a competition held in Malaysia before the X Games, is invited, too. The remaining skaters are invited because they are ranked highly by the ASA, or because they performed well in competitions such as the ASA World Championships. In women's events, the winners of the most recent X Games and the ASA World Championships qualify. The ASA picks the other women skaters based on rankings and the results of other in-line competitions.

The 1st X-Games In-Line Competition

There were six in-line skating events at 1995's Extreme Games. Australian Tom Fry won the men's vert event. Tash Hodgeson of New Zealand won the women's vert event. "Vert" is short for **vertical**. In the vert event, the athletes skate up and down a giant, *U*-shaped **half-pipe**. Another in-line event at the Extreme Games was the park event. In this event, athletes do a **routine** of tricks while skating in a skate park.

B. "Love" Hardin, a Texan, won the best trick event. His trick was to glide along the outside of the 25 foot (7.5 m) rail in the skate park! Derek Downing of Georgia won the 1995 men's downhill event. Chris Edwards, a skater from Minnesota who has created many aggressive in-line tricks, won the high-air event. These three in-line skating events are no longer in the X Games.

Matt Salerno of Australia won the men's park event at the Extreme Games in 1995. Salerno is a very well known skater and still competes today.

*Takeshi Yasutoko of Japan performed a tricky move on the half-pipe
at an event in Lake Havasu, Arizona, in March, 2000.*

Great Moments at the X Games

The 1999 X Games in San Francisco, California, was the first X Games for 15-year-old Nicky Adams of Montreal, Canada. Adams did a lot of midair spins without falling. He won the gold medal. Adams was so excited about winning that he did cartwheels on the course!

In the women's vert event in 1999, 14-year-old Ayumi Kawasaki of Japan beat 20-year-old Fabiola da Silva. Da Silva had won the women's vert event in 1996, 1997, and 1998. Kawasaki ended da Silva's winning streak!

The men's vert event at the 2000 X Games in San Francisco was a great event for the Yasutoko family of Japan. Sixteen-year-old Eito won that event's gold medal for the second year in a row. His 14-year-old brother, Takeshi, won the silver medal. It is not surprising that these brothers are talented skaters. Their father owns a skate park in Japan!

13

A Star In-Line Skater at the X Games

Fabiola da Silva is the leading aggressive in-line skater today. She has won seven X-Games medals, more than any other in-line skater. Da Silva won the gold medal in the women's vert event in 1996, 1997, 1998, 2000, and 2001. She also placed first in the women's park event at the 2000 X Games. Da Silva's other medal is a silver medal for the women's vert event in 1999.

Da Silva is such a great athlete that in 2000 the ASA passed the "Fabiola Rule." This rule lets her and other women compete in the men's in-line vert event if they qualify. "I just want to show that girls can do anything they want to," da Silva says.

Fabiola da Silva of Brazil is one of the best in-line skaters in the world. Here she is in Encinitas, California, balancing with one hand on the edge of a half-pipe.

15

16

Matt Salerno leaps over an obstacle during the park finals at the 2001 X Games in Philadelphia, Pennsylvania. The obstacles include ramps, stairs, and handrails.

The Park Event

The park event course has **obstacles** such as **quarter-pipes**. The course is 160 feet (49 m) by 130 feet (40 m). In this event's first round, 26 competitors each do two 60-second runs. Each athlete tries to impress the crowd and the judges with his or her tricks, such as spins and **backflips**. These tricks can be done anywhere on the course. At the end of the round, the athlete's two scores are **averaged**. The 10 male athletes with the best scores move on to the men's final round. Only the five best-scoring women skate in the women's park finals. More men make the finals because there are more male skaters than female skaters in the world.

In both the men's and the women's finals of the park event, the skaters do two more 60-second runs. Each skater's highest score is counted as his or her final score.

The Vert Event

The half-pipe that the athletes skate on during the vert event is 12 ½ feet (4 m) high and 56 feet (17 m) wide. The size of the pipe allows the skaters to fly high in the air above it!

In the first round of the men's vert event, each invited vert athlete does two 45-second runs. The skater's two scores are averaged, and the 10 best skaters advance to the final round. Two more 45-second runs are done in the final round. The better of these two scores is the skater's final score.

The women's vert event usually has just four skaters, so the first round is also the final round. At the 2001 X Games, the ASA decided that only Fabiola da Silva and Ayumi Kawasaki were qualified to skate in that event. Da Silva beat Kawasaki. No third-place women's vert medal was awarded that year.

Javier Bujanda soars high above the half-pipe in the vert event.

A Talk with Matt Lindenmuth

Matt "Lindy" Lindenmuth is an aggressive in-line skater from Kutztown, Pennsylvania. He was born on March 1, 1981. Lindy has skated in the X-Games in-line vert event every year since 1997. His best X-Games vert skating performance was in 1999, when he came in fourth place at the X Games in San Francisco.

What does it feel like to skate in the X Games?
The energy that I get from the crowd is the best fuel in the world. It's like tapping into a power source that enables you to try anything.

How do you prepare for a run?
Before I get to the ramp, I **compile** a list of my tricks and memorize my "line." Then, before I get on deck, I go off by myself, listen to my favorite music, focus my energy, and relax.

Matt "Lindy" Lindenmuth ▶

What has been your favorite X-Games moment?
Landing my double backflip at the 2001 X Games in Philly in front of my hometown crowd.

What do you think will be ahead for aggressive in-line skating at future X Games?
Bigger tricks. More height in skaters' air. Faster skating. More spins. More flips. Basically, I see things being elevated up a notch from where they are now.

What's your advice to kids who would like to try aggressive in-line skating?
Have fun! Make good friends, and love to roll!

What's Ahead for In-Line Skating

The ASA says that in-line skating is the fastest-growing sport in the world. The ASA also says that in-line skating is the most popular sport among young men in the United States today. In-line skating certainly has come a long way since it began to catch the world's attention in the early 1980s!

There is no reason to think that in-line skating's huge growth will stop anytime soon. Extreme sporting events such as the X Games help to make in-line skating more popular every year. That's great news for every in-line skater and fan out there.

Glossary

aggressive (uh-GREH-siv) Bold and active.

Aggressive Skaters Association (uh-GRES-iv SKAYT-erz ah-soh-see-AY-shun) The group that makes the rules for aggressive in-line skating.

athletes (ATH-leets) People who take part in sports.

averaged (A-vrijd) Put together to find the number that is in between the two scores.

backflips (BAK-flips) Tricks where skaters spin upside down in the air.

competition (kom-pih-TIH-shin) A sports contest.

compile (kom-PYL) To put together.

extreme sport (ek-STREEM SPORT) A sport such as aggressive in-line skating, skateboarding, motocross, wakeboarding, bicycle stunt riding, and street luge.

half-pipe (HAF-pyp) A ramp that is shaped like a big *U*.

international (in-tur-NA-shuh-nul) Including different countries of the world.

medals (MED-lz) Small, round pieces of metal that are given as awards.

midair (mid-AYR) Happening in the air

obstacles (OB-stuh-kulz) Items put on the skate park course such as ramps or pipes.

qualify (KWAH-lih-fy) To meet the requirements of something.

quarter-pipes (KWOR-tur-pyps) Ramps that look like halves of half-pipes.

routine (roo-TEEN) The series of tricks an athlete does during a run.

vertical (VER-tih-kul) In an up-and-down direction.

Index

A
Adams, Nicky, 13
Aggressive Skaters Association
    (ASA), 9, 14, 18, 22
ASA Pro Tour, 9
ASA World Championships, 9

D
da Silva, Fabiola, 6, 13, 14,
    18
Downing, Derek, 10

E
Edwards, Chris, 10

F
"Fabiola Rule", 14

Fry, Tom, 10

H
Hardin, B. "Love", 10
Hodgeson, Tash, 10

K
Kawasaki, Ayumi, 13, 18
Kutztown, PA, 20

L
Lindenmuth, Matt "Lindy", 20

M
medal(s), 6, 13, 14, 18

P
park event, 10, 14, 17

R
Rhode Island, 6

S
San Francisco, California, 13,
    20

V
vert event, 10, 13, 14, 18,
    20

Y
Yasutoko, Eito, 13
Yasutoko, Takeshi, 13

Web Sites

Due to the changing nature of Internet links, PowerKids Press has developed an online list of Web sites related to the subject of this book. This site is updated regularly. Please use this link to access the list:
www.powerkidslinks.com/kgxg/inlninx